Pebble®

**Out in Space**

# The Planets

by Martha E. H. Rustad

Consulting Editor: Gail Saunders-Smith, PhD

Consultant: Roger D. Launius, PhD
Senior Curator, Division of Space History
National Air and Space Museum
Smithsonian Institution, Washington, D.C.

Capst

Mankato, Min

Pebble Books are published by Capstone Press,
151 Good Counsel Drive, P.O. Box 669, Mankato, Minnesota 56002.
www.capstonepress.com

1 2 3 4 5 6 13 12 11 10 09 08

*Library of Congress Cataloging-in-Publication Data*
Rustad, Martha E. H. (Martha Elizabeth Hillman), 1975–
   The planets / by Martha E. H. Rustad. — Rev. and updated.
   p. cm. — (Pebble Books. Out in space)
   Summary: "Photographs and simple text introduce the planets in our solar
system" — Provided by publisher.
   Includes bibliographical references and index.
   ISBN-13: 978-1-4296-1719-2 (hardcover)
   ISBN-10: 1-4296-1719-5 (hardcover)
   ISBN-13: 978-1-4296-2814-3 (softcover)
   ISBN-10: 1-4296-2814-6 (softcover)
   1. Planets — Juvenile literature. I. Title.
QB602.R86 2009
523.4 — dc22                                     2007051305

## Note to Parents and Teachers

The Out in Space set provides the most up-to-date solar system
information to support national science standards. This book
describes and illustrates the planets. The photographs support
early readers in understanding the text. This book also introduces
early readers to subject-specific vocabulary words, which are
defined in the Glossary section. Early readers may need assistance
to read some words and to use the Table of Contents, Glossary,
Read More, Internet Sites, and Index sections of the book.

# Table of Contents

4

# Earth

Earth is the third planet
from the Sun.
You can see Earth's
water and land
from space.

Sun

Earth

A planet is a large object
that moves around the Sun.
Earth moves around
the Sun once each year.

Sun

Mercury

Venus

Moon

Earth

Mars

Asteroid Belt

Ceres
(dwarf planet)

Jupiter

Saturn

Uranus

Neptune

Pluto
(dwarf planet)

Eris
(dwarf planet)

8

# The Solar System

Planets, dwarf planets, asteroids, and comets move around the Sun. These objects and the Sun make up the solar system.

Jupiter

Saturn

Neptune

Uranus

Jupiter, Saturn,
Uranus, and Neptune
are large planets.
They are made
of gases.

**Earth**

**Mars**

**Mercury**

**Venus**

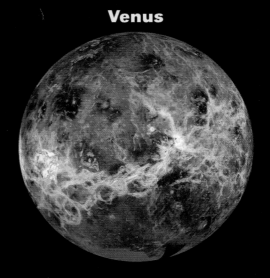

Earth, Mars,
Mercury, and Venus
are smaller planets.
They are rocky.

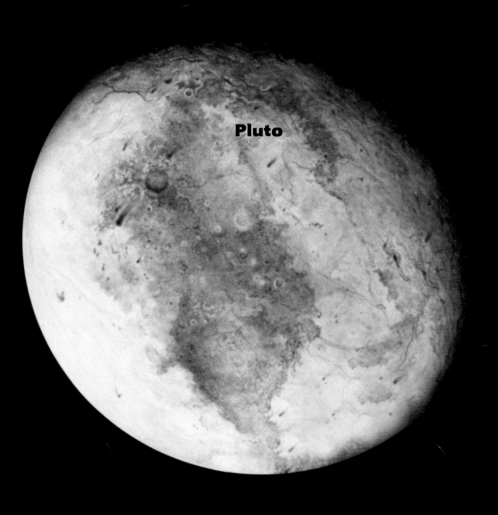

Pluto

Pluto, Ceres, and Eris
are smaller than planets.
They are dwarf planets.
Dwarf planets are
made of rock and ice.

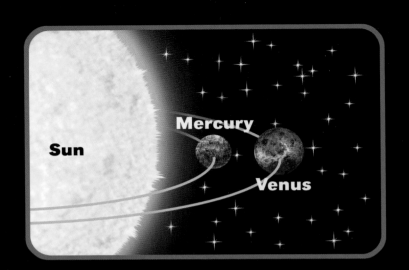

Sun

Mercury

Venus

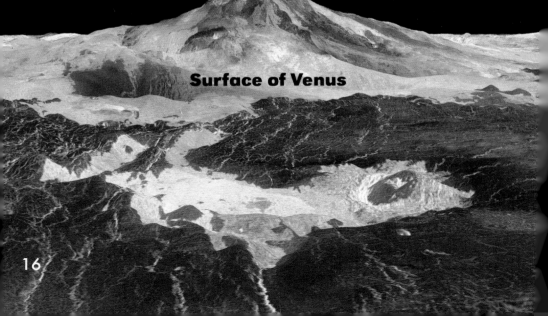

**Surface of Venus**

# Distance from the Sun

Mercury and Venus
are close to the Sun.
These planets are
very hot.

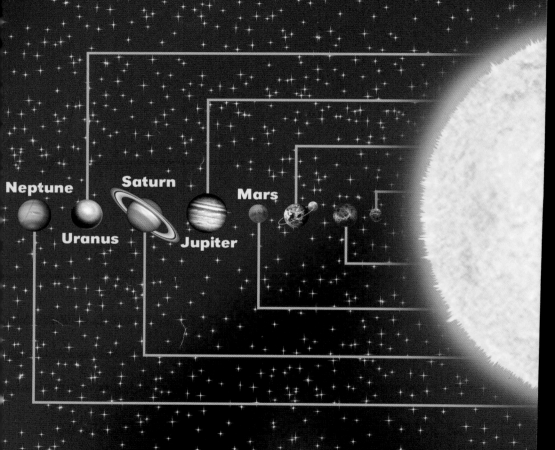

**Neptune**

**Uranus**

**Saturn**

**Jupiter**

**Mars**

Mars, Jupiter, Saturn,
Uranus, and Neptune
are far from the Sun.
These planets are
very cold.

Earth's place near the Sun gives Earth light and heat. The Sun helps plants grow. Earth is just the right distance from the Sun.

# Glossary

**asteroid** — a large rocky body that moves around the Sun; asteroids are too small to be called planets.

**comet** — a ball of rock and ice that moves around the Sun

**dwarf planet** — a round object that moves around the Sun but is too small to be a planet; Pluto is a dwarf planet.

**gas** — a substance that spreads to fill any space that holds it

**solar system** — the Sun and the objects that move around it; our solar system has eight planets, dwarf planets including Pluto, and many moons, asteroids, and comets.

**Sun** — the star that the planets and dwarf planets move around; the Sun provides light and heat to the planets and dwarf planets.

# Read More

**Adamson, Thomas K.** *Pluto: A Dwarf Planet.* Exploring the Galaxy. Mankato, Minn.: Capstone Press, 2008.

**Bredeson, Carmen.** *What Is the Solar System?* I Like Space! Berkeley Heights, N.J.: Enslow, 2008.

**Gibbons, Gail.** *The Planets.* New York: Holiday House, 2008.

# Internet Sites

FactHound offers a safe, fun way to find Internet sites related to this book. All of the sites on FactHound have been researched by our staff.

Here's how:

1. Visit *www.facthound.com*

2. Choose your grade level.

3. Type in this book ID **1429617195** for age-appropriate sites. You may also browse subjects by clicking on letters, or by clicking on pictures and words.

4. Click on the **Fetch It** button.

**FactHound will fetch the best sites for you!**

# Index

asteroids, 9
Ceres, 15
comets, 9
dwarf planets, 9, 15
Earth, 5, 7, 13, 21
Eris, 15
gases, 11
Jupiter, 11, 19
Mars, 13, 19

Mercury, 13, 17
Neptune, 11, 19
Pluto, 15
Saturn, 11, 19
solar system, 9
Sun, 5, 7, 9, 17, 19, 21
Uranus, 11, 19
Venus, 13, 17

Word Count: 153
Grade: 1
Early-Intervention Level: 15

**Editorial Credits**
Katy Kudela, revised edition editor; Kim Brown, designer and illustrator; Jo Miller, photo researcher

**Photo Credits**
Digital Vision, cover; NASA, 14; NASA/JPL, 1; NASA/JPL, 8 (Neptune and Venus); NASA/JPL, 10 (Neptune); NASA/JPL, 12 (Venus); NASA/JPL, 16 (both Venus images); NASA/JPL, 18 (Neptune and Venus); NASA/STScI, 8 (Jupiter and Saturn); NASA/STScI, 10 (Jupiter and Saturn); NASA/STScI, 18 (Jupiter and Saturn); NASA/USGS, 8 (Mars and Uranus); NASA/USGS, 10 (Uranus); NASA/USGS, 12 (Mars); NASA/USGS, 18 (Mars and Uranus); NASA/USGS/GOES, 4; NASA/Visible Earth, 8 (Earth); NASA/Visible Earth, 12 (Earth); NASA/Visible Earth, 18 (Earth); Photodisc, 8 (Mercury); Photodisc, 12 (Mercury); Photodisc, 16 (Mercury); Photodisc, 18 (Mercury); Shutterstock/Wojciech, 20